A Common Vision

by Neena Beber

A SAMUEL FRENCH ACTING EDITION

NEW YORK HOLLYWOOD LONDON TORONTO

SAMUELFRENCH.COM

Copyright © 2009 by Neena Beber

ALL RIGHTS RESERVED

CAUTION: Professionals and amateurs are hereby warned that *A COMMON VISION* is subject to a Licensing Fee. It is fully protected under the copyright laws of the United States of America, the British Commonwealth, including Canada, and all other countries of the Copyright Union. All rights, including professional, amateur, motion picture, recitation, lecturing, public reading, radio broadcasting, television and the rights of translation into foreign languages are strictly reserved. In its present form the play is dedicated to the reading public only.

The amateur live stage performance rights to *A COMMON VISION* are controlled exclusively by Samuel French, Inc., and licensing arrangements and performance licenses must be secured well in advance of presentation. PLEASE NOTE that amateur Licensing Fees are set upon application in accordance with your producing circumstances. When applying for a licensing quotation and a performance license please give us the number of performances intended, dates of production, your seating capacity and admission fee. Licensing Fees are payable one week before the opening performance of the play to Samuel French, Inc., at 45 W. 25th Street, New York, NY 10010.

Licensing Fee of the required amount must be paid whether the play is presented for charity or gain and whether or not admission is charged.

Stock licensing fees quoted upon application to Samuel French, Inc.

For all other rights than those stipulated above, apply to: SUBIAS, One Union Square West, No. 913, New York, NY 10003, Attn: Mark Subias.

Particular emphasis is laid on the question of amateur or professional readings, permission and terms for which must be secured in writing from Samuel French, Inc.

Copying from this book in whole or in part is strictly forbidden by law, and the right of performance is not transferable.

Whenever the play is produced the following notice must appear on all programs, printing and advertising for the play: "Produced by special arrangement with Samuel French, Inc."

Due authorship credit must be given on all programs, printing and advertising for the play.

ISBN 978-0-573-69661-9   Printed in U.S.A.   #29070

No one shall commit or authorize any act or omission by which the copyright of, or the right to copyright, this play may be impaired.

No one shall make any changes in this play for the purpose of production.

Publication of this play does not imply availability for performance. Both amateurs and professionals considering a production are strongly advised in their own interests to apply to Samuel French, Inc., for written permission before starting rehearsals, advertising, or booking a theatre.

No part of this book may be reproduced, stored in a retrieval system, or transmitted in any form, by any means, now known or yet to be invented, including mechanical, electronic, photocopying, recording, videotaping, or otherwise, without the prior written permission of the publisher.

IMPORTANT BILLING AND CREDIT REQUIREMENTS

All producers of *A COMMON VISION* must give credit to the Author of the Play in all programs distributed in connection with performances of the Play, and in all instances in which the title of the Play appears for the purposes of advertising, publicizing or otherwise exploiting the Play and/or a production. The name of the Author *must* appear on a separate line on which no other name appears, immediately following the title and *must* appear in size of type not less than fifty percent of the size of the title type.

In addition the following credit *must* be given in all programs and publicity information distributed in association with this piece:

A COMMON VISION was first produced by The Magic Theatre (artistic director - Larry Eilenberg; managing director - Dianne M. Terp).

A COMMON VISION was written with the support of an Amblin Commission from Playwrights Horizons.

A COMMON VISION was first produced by The Magic Theatre (artistic director - Larry Eilenberg; managing director - Dianne M. Terp). It was directed by Mary Coleman, with sets by Mikiko Uesugi, lighting by York Kennedy, costumes by Callie Floor, sound by Gregory Kohn, casting director Amanda Duarte, and stage management by Robert Earl Webb. The cast was as follows:

DOLORES . . . . Anne Darragh
ELIOTT . . . . Warren D. Keith
JANINE . . . . Sally Dana
RICHARD . . . . John Flanagan
JIM . . . . Eric Siegel
MONA . . . . Amy Resnick

CHARACTERS

DOLORES – A woman on the fourteenth floor
ELIOTT – An expert
JANINE – An artist
RICHARD – A witness
JIM – A witness
MONA – A neighbor

PLACE

A city with tall buildings

To my dad, Dr. Charles Robert Beber,
who always told the best stories,
and who is my hero.

(It's the middle of the night. A single light shines on **DOLORES**. *She hovers mid-air. She wears a white night-gown. The night-gown flutters around her as she floats up. The beam of light brightens.)*

DOLORES. Please let me remember this. I want to remember. Will I remember this? Because I want, I want to remember. Please God let me remember.

(Blackout on **DOLORES**. *Lights up on two men,* **RICHARD** *and* **JIM**, *standing on the street below. They wear dark suits, like secret service men.)*

RICHARD. I need to whiz.

*(***JIM** *looks up, then* **RICHARD**. *They see* **DOLORES** *floating in the sky, suspended by…nothing.)*

JIM. Jesus.

RICHARD. God.

(Black-out. Lights up on an apartment living room. **DOLORES** *enters from her bedroom wearing the white nightgown. She's disoriented. She makes tea. She stares at the phone, waits for the water to boil.)*

DOLORES. *(to telephone)* You bastard.

(The tea kettle whistles. She turns off the kettle, pours her tea, and goes back to staring at the phone.)

DOLORES. Bastard. You bastard. Bastard.

(She goes for the phone and dials.)

DOLORES. *(into phone)* You've ruined my life. Yes, yes, that's how I feel. I feel that you've ruined my life. Don't tell me how I feel. You can't tell me how I feel, I know how I feel, and I feel that you've ruined my life. Yes you have. That is bullshit, we are responsible *for each other*, okay? Don't give me that, we are all *responsible* for each *other* don't hang up on me. Don't hang up on me, I'm hanging up on you first. Don't hang up.

(She hangs up the phone. Looks at it. When the phone rings, she grabs it.)

DOLORES. *(into phone)* WHAT DO YOU WANT FROM ME? Oh, sorry, Mona. Bastard. Do you think he'll call back? I hung up on him. Maybe I shouldn't have. Do you think I shouldn't have? You can come upstairs but I'm not getting dressed today. I've decided I'm not getting dressed today. That *is* what I'm doing for myself: I'm not getting dressed. Because I don't feel like it. All right.

(She hangs up the phone.)

God help me. God help me. God help me. God. *(to phone)* Call me back you fuck, you fucking bastard, call me.

*(She hears steps outside, opens door to **MONA**. **MONA** holds out two danishes, carries a tabloid paper.)*

MONA. Eat something.

DOLORES. I can't.

MONA. You should eat something. Are you eating?

DOLORES. I'm not hungry.

MONA. Did you sleep at all last night? You look terrible.

DOLORES. Thanks.

MONA. This over an asshole.

DOLORES. Loser.

MONA. Suckhole.

DOLORES. Loser suckhole bastard fuck. I loved him. I really loved him. I still love him WHY. I'm not getting over him. I should be getting over him but I'm not. I pray to get over him. I don't pray for him to come back, I pray to get over him, that's a step in the right direction, isn't it?

MONA. Ellen's on Prozac. She feels wonderful. She looks fantastic.

DOLORES. What's your point?

MONA. That married man she was waiting around for, eight years, something like that? Now he comes begging she doesn't want him anymore. The window of opportunity has slammed shut, she says. Little Ellen says that. Slam, and that was some window. Eight years I'd say isn't just a window, it's a sliding glass door. Can I have a cup of, what is that, coffee?

DOLORES. *(pours her a cup)* Church. It's tea. I've got to go to church. I need church.

MONA. I met this man last night, and I…

DOLORES. That's great, you met someone.

MONA. I slept with this man I met last night. Maybe I should go to church, too. This tea is cold. Some kind of diplomat. He was important, I think. He had security guards. He won't call.

DOLORES. You don't know that.

MONA. Anyway he wasn't my type. *(reading tabloid)* Rosanne's on Prozac. Look how great Roseanne looks.

DOLORES. Do you know of a church I might go to?

MONA. Of course she's had a lot of plastic surgery. I haven't been to church since I was a little girl.

DOLORES. I used to go. I used to pray.

MONA. Except as a tourist. The churches were always empty. They must keep the real churches hidden from the tourists.

DOLORES. Can I just go? Do you need a membership? Some kind of church membership? Can a person just show up off the street?

MONA. That's what church is for. So do you want me to go with you?

DOLORES. That's all right.

MONA. Maybe I should.

DOLORES. I need to go alone. I need to be a stranger, all alone, and I need to walk in, as inconspicuously as possible, and I need to find a little pew, and I need to pray. I need to pray somewhere. That's what I need to do. It doesn't matter where just not here. Do you need to pay to go to church?

MONA. They might pass around a plate.

DOLORES. I don't think he's going to call. That's okay. Not call. Okay, there are worse things, people deal with far worse – I'll just pick one, the first one I pass, I pass them all the time. I don't care what denomination. The first one I pass, that's where I'll go.

*(**DOLORES** puts a coat on over her nightgown.)*

MONA. If you're not having that danish –

DOLORES. Go ahead.

MONA. Unless you're going to have it.

DOLORES. Finish it.

MONA. It's very good danish.

DOLORES. I'm going to church.

*(**DOLORES** exits. Outside. She takes out a cell phone and dials.)*

DOLORES. *(into phone)* Are you fucking somebody else? Is that it? Fuck you if you're fucking somebody else. My body isn't even cold yet. IT ISN'T EVEN COLD. How can you be fucking somebody else already, *are* you? Just tell me I want to know. Just tell me.

(shifting tone; sweetly now)

Tell me the truth I'll be fine with it really, really I'm okay, just tell me.

(shifting back)

FUCK YOU if you can't even tell me. You're fucking somebody else, fuck you.

(She throws down the phone. She goes to a pew in a church and prays.)

*(Lights up on **ELIOTT** and **JANINE** in a cafe.)*

JANINE. I don't think that people can be fixed – cured. What are you even curing? That you help them…I no longer believe that you help them.

ELIOTT. You may be right.

JANINE. You're agreeing with me?

ELIOTT. I've spent too many years trying to help turn hysterical misery into ordinary unhappiness, as Freud said – well, I'd like to do better than that.

JANINE. Do you think it's possible? To "do better"?

ELIOTT. I hope so. I've been delving into other areas. I've been looking for a way to give a spiritual component to the work.

JANINE. Spiritual. That's a new word for you, no?

(**DOLORES** *prays.*)

DOLORES. God…dear God…let me run into him. If I could just run into him. People run into people why can't I just…I'm asking so little. To see his face. I think I could feel whole again if I could just see his face Tom…Tom.

ELIOTT. It's not just inside us, in here…it's out there, do you see? Something is out there.

(**JANINE** *takes a sip of her drink.*)

JANINE. This is quite strong for the middle of the day.

ELIOTT. We'll send it back.

JANINE. No. Thanks.

ELIOTT. I miss you, Janine. I really miss you.

JANINE. Are you saying you want me back?

ELIOTT. No. I guess I'm not saying that.

JANINE. All right. Good.

ELIOTT. How are things going with – what's his name?

JANINE. They're fine, actually. Hal. They're fine. Cynthia?

ELIOTT. Mmm. You still look beautiful, you know.

JANINE. "Still." Is that really necessary, to say "still" like that?

ELIOTT. I always knew you'd get over me.

JANINE. Yes. Well. You were right. Time heals all.

ELIOTT. You think so?

JANINE. What?

ELIOTT. Time heals all?

JANINE. We just don't live long enough. If we could live a hundred, two hundred, a thousand years…eventually all would be healed.

ELIOTT. Mmm...

(**JANINE** *rises abruptly.*)

JANINE. Well I'm so glad we got together.

ELIOTT. Are you?

JANINE. Wonderful idea, yes, I'm so glad you called.

ELIOTT. Are you.

JANINE. I better – meeting Hal and so on – thanks so much.

(**JANINE** *starts to go.*)

ELIOTT. Janine?

JANINE. Yes?

ELIOTT. I think of you.

JANINE. That's nice. That's very nice. How nice that you think of me.

(**JANINE** *goes.* **DOLORES** *sits alone in* **ELIOTT**'s *office.* **ELIOTT** *enters scene. He listens.*)

DOLORES. The Greeks had it right. It's a bunch of petty little gods up there and they're *fucking* with us, they're just *fucking* with us. That's what I think. We're their fodder. Human fodder. You're in favor, you're out of favor, you're fucked, you're...you're...I'm destroyed. There's nothing left. There's no one sitting here. There's nothing sitting here. I'm a slab of pain. That's all. That's all. Do you mind if I smoke?

ELIOTT. Please.

DOLORES. I won't light it. I just need...

ELIOTT. To hold something?

DOLORES. Yes. Is there a pill? If there's a pill for heartache, I'll take it.

ELIOTT. I'd like to explore some other options first.

DOLORES. "Options." That makes it sound like I have some say in, in these things in my life.

ELIOTT. You feel – how do you feel?

(**DOLORES** *shrugs.*)

Helpless?

DOLORES. I'm like one of those geese. The way baby geese follow around the first face they see? That's all it takes to make them follow that face everywhere: one look. Tom's face is in my brain like that. Imprinted, is that the word?

ELIOTT. I think you know that it is. *(beat)* You're in a lot of pain.

DOLORES. Obviously.

ELIOTT. You feel that this man – that he is the source of your pain.

DOLORES. Oh, Jesus. The source, okay, like way back, like I don't really care, okay? He is the source in this sense, in the sense that I was happy, and now he has left me and I am unhappy. It's very simple, see?

ELIOTT. Were you?

DOLORES. What?

ELIOTT. Happy…before him.

DOLORES. Before he left me or before I ever met him?

ELIOTT. Either one.

DOLORES. I've been happy. Of course. And we were happy together. I think we were.

ELIOTT. Because if you were, then you have that capacity: to *be* happy. There are people who come to me who don't even feel that they have that.

DOLORES. Over a period of time he took a chisel, a chisel to my soul and he chipped away gradually, gently, until there was nothing left – gently chiseling – wearing down one's center.

ELIOTT. And this is the person you want back?

DOLORES. God, I hate this.

(Lights up on **JIM** *and* **RICHARD**.*)*

JIM. "The woman in question was wearing a white night-gown. She appeared to hover somewhere between the eleventh floor and the top of said building. The time was approximately 3:52 AM."

(**DOLORES** *and* **ELIOTT**, *still in their scene.*)

ELIOTT. Is it that you hate being probed like this?

DOLORES. Probed? I don't know. What a funny word. Do I hate being probed. Wouldn't anyone? Yes.

(**ELIOTT** *looks at* **DOLORES**. *She takes off coat; in the white nightgown, she appears behind* **JIM** *and* **RICHARD**.)

JIM. The woman in question wore a white nightgown. She wore white. She wore white. She wore a white nightgown.

RICHARD. You're repeating yourself, Jim. Why are you repeating yourself, Jim?

JIM. It's important to get it right.

RICHARD. A woman floated out of her apartment, her high-rise apartment, and got sucked up on a beam of light. Disappeared into the light. End of story, there you have it.

JIM. The woman wore a white nightgown.

RICHARD. Is that relevant?

JIM. The nightgown was…it was white. It was so light. And the woman, she…she had her own light.

RICHARD. Let's just file the report, shall we?

JIM. Do you think she's okay?

RICHARD. This is a situation, Jim. That we're in the middle of. And I'm not sure how I feel about that.

JIM. I need to know if she's okay.

RICHARD. I prefer not to be involved in a situation such as this.

JIM. We already are involved. What made you look up, Rich? We looked up. It must mean something. What does it mean?

RICHARD. Facts, Jim.

JIM. Fact: people don't float up, they fall down. Fact: people don't fly. They don't disappear into the sky. Into the night. She appeared, then *dis*-appeared. Where did she go, Rich? Fuck facts.

RICHARD. We are going to need to think clearly here. We were on duty. We were protecting a very important figure. He asked us to wait outside. He was in the building at the time. People will ask why he was in the building at the time. His dealings are very private. That wouldn't be good, Jim. For people to ask that.

JIM. I think my wife's been having an affair.

RICHARD. Sorry to hear that, Jim.

JIM. Do you know how that feels, to have to picture that?

RICHARD. Move on or move out, that's my policy.

JIM. You've never lived with anyone.

RICHARD. That is correct. Why? People betray you. They can't help it. It's in their natures, programmed right into the DNA: to betray. At the very least they drop dead. Who needs that. I don't.

JIM. You've never even had a girlfriend. Unless you're just very private. Are you just very private, Rich?

RICHARD. I'll write up the report.

JIM. I want to do it. I looked up first, I saw her first.

RICHARD. That sounds a bit childish, Jim.

JIM. Woman in white nightgown. White. Flying up into the light like that. I need to know…if she's okay.

(**DOLORES** *enters scene with* **MONA**. **MONA** *has danishes again, and a tabloid.*)

MONA. Why do people care what you do when they're not looking?

DOLORES. What?

MONA. My boss doesn't want me to read magazines at work. They're on my lap, my lap is under my desk, what does he care?

DOLORES. It's probably a policy. I called in sick again.

MONA. It might make you feel better to go to work.

DOLORES. I know. I tell myself that, but I just can't – go.

MONA. We need an idea, you know what I'm saying? We need a really big idea that will make us a lot of money

MONA. *(cont.)* really fast. Like Liquid Paper, that was just some secretary's idea, cover your mistakes with white nail polish. A million dollars for that.

DOLORES. I'll collect unemployment if they fire me, I hope they do.

MONA. Did you know that the inventor of Liquid Paper was the mother of one of the Monkees? The TV rock star guys? Do some people have all the luck or what?

DOLORES. He owes me money. I'm throwing out his stuff. He left a sweater here, it's not even a nice sweater, and he owes me, like, two hundred bucks. I figured that out; I was calculating who spent what on what and he's ahead by two hundred. Shouldn't I get that back?

MONA. Can't he give you a pill?

DOLORES. We're exploring other options.

MONA. I think you should try to get a pill.

(**DOLORES** *enters scene with* **ELIOTT**.)

ELIOTT. And your sleep...are you sleeping well?

DOLORES. I don't know.

ELIOTT. How is that, "don't know"?

DOLORES. When I wake up it's as if I've been...absent, somehow. More dead than asleep. Somehow.

ELIOTT. Any trouble with memory?

DOLORES. I'm not sure.

ELIOTT. Do you forget things?

DOLORES. How do you know if you've forgotten something if you can't remember it in the first place?

ELIOTT. Okay. But there's a sensation of missing time?

DOLORES. *Something* missing, anyway. Like a photo album with the snapshots gone blurry.

ELIOTT. That's nice, let's go with that. You can't see the pictures in your head, but you know they're there?

DOLORES. They're all blurry, and sometimes...torn out. Whole pages. It's like I remember Tom more than myself...better than myself. I remember going places, how he was, what he saw, but…where was I? Did he just tell me or was I there? I can't always remember if I was there. But of course you can't see yourself actually, so you can't remember yourself, in that way. *(beat)* Oh.

ELIOTT. What is it, Dolores?

DOLORES. I just remembered something.

ELIOTT. Tell me.

DOLORES. My dreams. I used to remember my dreams.

ELIOTT. And you just remembered one?

DOLORES. No, I remembered that I forget them. Now when I wake up, they're gone. Tom and I used to tell each other our dreams. Everyone dreams, right? I must still have them.

*(**DOLORES** backs away. Into her apartment, on phone.)*

DOLORES. *(into phone)* Tom? Tom, it's me, pick up? It's me. I'm feeling better. I'm really much better. Maybe we should get together. Maybe we should get together some time if you have time. Maybe that would be nice. Are you there, Tom? Are you there with someone else? It's okay, it's –

*(**MONA** comes in, looks at her. **DOLORES** hangs up phone.)*

MONA. Want to hear your horoscope? Let me read you this, Dee, it's good: "Cease waiting for others to change, and make a few alterations yourself. Time away from a spouse or lover brings home just how much he or she means to you. Avoid impulsive spending."

DOLORES. That's good? That sucks.

MONA. "Time away from a lover brings home just how much he means to you" – why isn't that good?

DOLORES. I already know how much he means to me, what good does that do? What about him, what does his say?

MONA. What is he?

DOLORES. Cancer.

MONA. Perfect. *(reads his to herself)* Oh, who cares about him. Want to hear mine?

DOLORES. Read Cancer.

MONA. "A passionate outing leads to lasting love. Popularity soars. Luck involves a refund."

DOLORES. Shit.

MONA. Fuck him.

DOLORES. Everything is good for him, and everything sucks for me.

MONA. You don't believe in horoscopes.

DOLORES. The stars are in his favor right now. Me they're fucking with. I lost my job, by the way.

MONA. We should go someplace together. Club Med, I've always wanted to go to one of those. Do you think they're too expensive, Club Med?

DOLORES. He's going to hypnotize me.

MONA. Ooh, creepy.

DOLORES. I'm afraid. I don't know why, I'm afraid.

(**DOLORES** *enters scene with* **ELIOTT**. *She speaks as if hypnotized. Stares out, stands on her toes, reaches up.*)

DOLORES. There is a tingling. My whole body...tingles...pins and needles...light flooding in from the window...so much light...I have to see, I have to...everything is spinning...

ELIOTT. What do you see, what?

DOLORES. Everything spinning...so much light...the sky...myself, the night...

ELIOTT. Where are you now?

DOLORES. There are children around me, little children, I'm afraid...

ELIOTT. Don't turn back, Dolores. You're safe. You're protected. Keep going. Keep seeing...what are you seeing?

DOLORES. I would hold them but I'm afraid...they might not be human they're small and pale I'm afraid...their eyes are so large. Such large eyes, they can see through me, see right through me...they want something from me I don't know what...I don't know if I'm awake I think I am...the night, dark, then suddenly light, so much light, everything spinning please God let me remember this I want, I want to remember...

(A scene shift. **DOLORES** *snaps to alertness, no longer under hypnosis.)*

DOLORES. Oh my God.

ELIOTT. Yes.

DOLORES. My God. It makes sense. When I was a little girl I used to think: people are watching me. Do most people have that feeling? Like, I'm in a movie, someone else's movie...everything I do is seen by somebody else, *for* somebody else.

ELIOTT. While now it may be true that you *are* in fact being watched and *have* been. It doesn't lessen the violation, but to have this concrete knowledge: it's not your imagination, it's real. It's real.

DOLORES. To have been chosen, against my will, probably from childhood...

ELIOTT. That's most often the case.

DOLORES. To have been impregnated, possibly, and aborted, possibly...all the missed periods, it makes sense, and the feeling of helplessness.

ELIOTT. But of course you *would* have felt that.

*(***DOLORES*** enters scene with* **MONA.** **MONA** *is reading a tabloid;* **DOLORES** *sees something on her hand.)*

MONA. Melanie Griffith's lips just keep getting bigger and bigger. What is she doing to herself?

*(***DOLORES*** shows* **MONA** *her hand.)*

DOLORES. Look.

MONA. What?

DOLORES. A scar. See it?

MONA. No.

DOLORES. Right here.

MONA. That?

DOLORES. It wasn't here before.

MONA. It's tiny, how would you know? You get lots of scars like that when you're a kid, then you forget them. Do you think I should get a tattoo?

DOLORES. Sure, if you want one.

MONA. I'm afraid if I get one I won't be able to stop. *(off magazine)* They call this woman the Tattoo Granny. She started with one little bird and then she just kept going. She says tattoos make her happy and I'd love to have a cute, tiny rose or dolphin or maybe a butterfly, but what if I can't stop? I'll end up getting tattoos all over my body, I'll end up looking like a freak.

DOLORES. You don't have to get one.

MONA. You're right, I better not.

(**DOLORES** *holds her hand out to* **ELIOTT**.)

DOLORES. It's a sign. A kind of proof, isn't it?

ELIOTT. Evidence of injury…but also of healing. When the wound heals, it leaves its mark.

DOLORES. I wonder what they, you know, what they did to me.

ELIOTT. We can't know for sure, but I believe that they have a purpose, Dolores. And I believe it will be to our benefit, in the end.

DOLORES. What if we never know? If we never know why we're here, or what they want from us.

ELIOTT. The question becomes a personal one, a way to make sense of our lives: how do I account for what is missing, what is out of my control and missing.

DOLORES. Because they took it. Is that what you mean, Dr. Turner?

ELIOTT. Eliott, please. The traditional hierarchical set-up doesn't make sense to me. We're two people struggling.

DOLORES. You struggle, then?

ELIOTT. We all struggle; that's the one thing we can count on. I've been looking for someone like you, Dolores.

DOLORES. Like me?

ELIOTT. Someone who has actually had this type of experience. We can investigate it together.

DOLORES. The missing piece of the puzzle.

ELIOTT. Suddenly found. You feel whole now…you're beginning to feel whole.

(DOLORES turns back to scene with MONA.)

DOLORES. There's been a void. Here is the thing. This feeling of emptiness, it isn't random. You see? There was a reason. A reason, Mona, something bigger than Tom, bigger than me…

MONA. Have you talked to Ellen yet? New person. Doesn't need a man anymore. Looks fantastic. She's focused on her career.

DOLORES. Her career as a temp worker?

MONA. She wants to start her own business. Little Ellen.

DOLORES. Listen, Mona, listen, I, in my work with Eliott, I –

MONA. "Eliott"?

DOLORES. It's not a conventional approach, it's…You're going to find all this difficult to believe.

(DOLORES joins ELIOTT in a television studio.)

DOLORES. At first I couldn't understand what was going on with me.

ELIOTT. You see she wasn't looking for this.

DOLORES. I really don't need this in my life.

ELIOTT. The people who come to me – and I believe they're sent to me, the ones who come without prior information but simply come to me because they are in crisis – they rarely even have any memory of this, initially. It's startling to everyone.

DOLORES. I came to him because I was in pain. I was hoping to get…a pill, actually. I thought it was my fault.

ELIOTT. Together we discovered that larger crisis.

DOLORES. It's difficult to accept.

ELIOTT. She has no reason to make this up.

DOLORES. My life would be easier without this knowledge; it's not how I want to be known.

ELIOTT. And yet now so many things come together.

DOLORES. Things I couldn't understand.

ELIOTT. People think of such silly things when they hear the term "UFO."

DOLORES. I certainly did.

ELIOTT. I myself was just beginning an inquiry. Our whole concept of reality, of purposefulness...all our categories must shift. Our whole notion that we are alone in the universe, whether by miracle or accident or natural design, is shattered.

DOLORES. I'm here to help others, others who are afraid to come forward, or who might not even realize...

ELIOTT. You see, in her human encounters she was struggling.

DOLORES. I was. I was struggling. I felt lost, really. I felt hopeless, I felt...I felt ashamed. All the time. It's hard to describe, really.

ELIOTT. UFO. Unidentified. But what helps is to identify – to identify that source of pain.

(DOLORES holds up her scar, looks at it. MONA turns to her.)

MONA. I think you're being influenced. You've been in a state, a very vulnerable state, and these ideas are being put into your head. By a wackadoo, if I do say so myself.

DOLORES. Eliott Turner is very distinguished.

MONA. You've been lonely and these ideas make you feel less lonely.

DOLORES. More lonely sometimes. More alone.

(RICHARD and JIM in ELIOTT's office.)

RICHARD. We agreed to come to you because you have a certain legitimacy. We did a lot of research.

JIM. We saw you on TV, actually.

RICHARD. That woman on TV –

JIM. We think she's the one we saw. We're not gullible people.

RICHARD. We're not, you know, your usual UFO people.

JIM. It's just that we know what we saw.

ELIOTT. I'm very glad that you came to me. When I read your report I felt that it called for, no, demanded a serious inquiry.

RICHARD. We don't take it lightly. We're in security, you know.

JIM. We keep people secure.

RICHARD. We protect very important people.

JIM. We can't name names.

RICHARD. Important people tend to be private. It's essential that we ourselves remain anonymous.

ELIOTT. I understand. As you know, I'm a classically trained psychoanalyst. I have a very distinguished practice.

RICHARD. Of course that's not why we're here.

ELIOTT. Of course not.

JIM. Psychiatric treatment, you know, some people might find that useful, we're not necessarily opposed as such…

RICHARD. But that's not our need, so to speak.

ELIOTT. No no, I just want to make clear –

JIM. Your credentials.

RICHARD. Which we're very impressed by.

ELIOTT. Thank you, but I mean the road, the road which has led me to believe in the truth of certain phenomena – UFOs, abductions, visitations – how it became clear to me that scientific exploration was warranted –

RICHARD. *Scientific*, exactly.

ELIOTT. Because I began to see in my practice, beginning with, with the woman you saw, certain evidence of, *trauma* perhaps is the best word I can come up with, a post-traumatic syndrome that could not be traced to the physical events of their childhood. There is a similar thread, a psychological thread if you will, connecting several of these patients and we began to uncover memories…this is what I've begun to research, what you're no doubt familiar with, the work I've begun on this subject.

JIM. People are frightened. That's our fear, that they're frightened.

ELIOTT. That's right, it took great courage on your part, on both your parts, to be willing to come forward. Men in your position and so on, credible men such as yourselves.

JIM. We want to do our duty.

RICHARD. We consider it a civic duty, though at this point we have drawn no conclusions.

ELIOTT. I'm simply here to listen.

RICHARD. We appreciate that.

ELIOTT. I want to hear your story.

JIM. That's what we're here to tell.

ELIOTT. Please. Let's begin.

(**ELIOTT** *turns on a tape recorder.*)

JIM. We were on duty.

RICHARD. It was sometime before dawn; in our estimation, 3:52 AM. We stood in front of the high rise…said high rise.

JIM. Along the East River. Richard had to whiz to tell you the truth.

RICHARD. In our profession you can't always retire to a facility, you understand. We hadn't been drinking.

JIM. Something made me look up…

(*The men fall out of scene as* **DOLORES** *replaces them, talking to* **ELIOTT**.)

ELIOTT. Apparently they were there.

DOLORES. They saw me.

ELIOTT. They witnessed the event.

DOLORES. I was seen.

ELIOTT. It's a reputable account.

DOLORES. So it's true.

ELIOTT. Did you doubt your own experience?

DOLORES. No, I…I guess I usually do.

ELIOTT. What's inside you is real, Dolores. Your story is real.

DOLORES. And I…I *was*, in *fact*, seen.

   *(**DOLORES** turns to **MONA**.)*

DOLORES. I don't think about Tom anymore.

MONA. You just did.

DOLORES. I wonder if he saw me.

MONA. Saw you where?

DOLORES. On TV.

MONA. I thought you meant you followed him somewhere again.

DOLORES. Maybe he heard about it. Somebody recognized me at the supermarket. She wanted my autograph.

MONA. Why?

DOLORES. She said she once saw a UFO and I helped her to feel okay about that.

MONA. So what's your autograph going to do for her?

DOLORES. Are you mad at me?

MONA. Of course not. Listen…No, forget it.

DOLORES. I hate it when you do that. What?

MONA. I met this guy, Edward.

DOLORES. You met someone?

MONA. Edward, this guy. And he wants a three-way. I think that's a common fantasy, don't you? He wants a three-way and I thought – you're my best friend and I thought –

DOLORES. Oh, Jesus.

MONA. I told you never mind. I just thought –

DOLORES. I have a lot to deal with right now.

MONA. We haven't done anything yet, but I think if I could offer him a three-way, just a one-shot deal, I think it might work out.

(ELIOTT in the cafe with JANINE.)

JANINE. The heart is like a flute.

ELIOTT. This is, um…?

JANINE. Something I read. Heartache and grief pierce holes through the heart…the way a flute needs holes to be played. So, so to make beautiful music one needs to experience pain.

ELIOTT. Mmn.

JANINE. That's lovely, isn't it?

ELIOTT. It's not something Hal said?

JANINE. No, it's not something Hal said.

ELIOTT. I'm glad we're meeting again. We can be friends now, right? Enough time has passed that we can be friends?

JANINE. I thought this was about work.

ELIOTT. Yes, I – I'd like for you to meet one of my patients.

JANINE. Your patients? Meet one? Is that proper?

ELIOTT. I'm writing a book.

JANINE. Well of course you would.

ELIOTT. I thought you might do the drawings. The illustrations. You might find it interesting.

JANINE. You want me to draw her?

ELIOTT. What she's seen. I think it could be helpful, for her as well. We don't have a photograph, obviously, and – you're so skillful when you draw. I can't understand why you choose to ignore those skills in your work.

JANINE. What about your skills? You were an analyst, an educator, and now – my God, I saw you on a talk show.

ELIOTT. How was I?

JANINE. Some daytime talk show. Really, isn't that beneath you?

ELIOTT. You were watching.

JANINE. I was flicking about.

ELIOTT. I want to reach people.

JANINE. UFOs, abductions, my God. You used to be so serious. I loved that about you. So serious. Such a snob, I loved that. Your wrote about nightmares, children's nightmares; grief states.

ELIOTT. If you could just meet her.

(**DOLORES** *replaces* **ELIOTT** *in the cafe.*)

DOLORES. A flute.

JANINE. Yes, well…I think it's Sufi. Or something.

DOLORES. And what if your heart gets punched through with so many holes there's nothing left? If a flute has too many holes, holes all over, you'll just get dead air, right?

JANINE. I guess I never thought about that.

DOLORES. You must be lucky then.

JANINE. No, I…just never thought about that. So. So, Eliott would like for me to help you visualize your…experience. You can think of me as a translator, I suppose.

DOLORES. Have you done this for him before?

JANINE. No, but when we were married, I – he didn't tell you?

DOLORES. No.

JANINE. Well, we're not anymore. Married. He was quite different then. He was very neurologically oriented.

DOLORES. Excuse me?

JANINE. His training, his academic –

DOLORES. I know what you're thinking: why would she be chosen? Why would anyone find her special? Why her?

JANINE. I would hardly say I was thinking that. Eliott hasn't asked me to meet anyone else before, by the way.

DOLORES. Oh. It's for his book…I'll be in his book.

JANINE. Yes, that's why I'm here. I just think it's a kind of mass hysteria.

DOLORES. I see.

JANINE. There's just not any good evidence, nothing of substance – there were faeries, there were elves, then witches, now there are UFOs. I'm not saying there isn't other life somewhere, at least the potential – I hope there is. I do see that you believe, that Eliott believes.

DOLORES. It's not a question of "belief."

JANINE. Isn't it?

DOLORES. Do you *believe* in trees? In sky, in milk, in the ocean? Do you believe that I'm sitting here talking to you now, do you believe what you see? Because I have witnesses. I was seen.

JANINE. I don't doubt that you "experienced" something, as Eliott likes to say.

DOLORES. What about light? What about air, the wind? What about the things you don't see? A feeling, maybe. A soul, maybe. Do you believe we have one?

JANINE. I suppose you *can* think of it that way.

DOLORES. Do you know what it's like to spend your whole life in heartache? Always longing for something and not knowing why, this hole, and then…then…it's like a gift, really.

JANINE. We're all homesick, all the time – if we're lucky enough to even know where home is.

DOLORES. You don't?

JANINE. I lived in different places.

DOLORES. Before you met Eliott.

JANINE. It's possible to transform pain. That's what I believe; to take your pain and transform it. In order to transcend it, ultimately. I believe that everyone has that capacity. And that that is more important – than dwelling, *dwelling* is what I used to call it, with El – with Eliott.

DOLORES. You're just a speck. Like me. Insignificant. But maybe, maybe we're important; maybe there's a plan and I'm included. You don't know what it feels like, you can't say. Because you've probably always felt that you *were* important, that you counted, mattered, you've probably *always*. Felt that way.

(**JIM** *waits in front of* **DOLORES**' *building. When she exits, he blocks her way.*)

JIM. Oh my God.

DOLORES. Excuse me?

JIM. Oh my God. You're all right. It's you, isn't it? You're all right.

DOLORES. Is there a problem? Do I know you? Is there a problem?

(to **ELIOTT***)* He came to me…he'd been waiting to see me…

JIM. You're all right. *(to* **RICHARD***)* I can't change what I've seen. It was because of what I had seen.

DOLORES. Can I help you? What is it that you want, can I *help* you?

JIM. Please…please, don't go, I…please don't go. I had to find you.

DOLORES. Find me? Who are you?

(He flashes his wallet.)

JIM. James Elwood. Security.

DOLORES. What is wrong is something wrong?

JIM. I was hoping to meet you, I need to know you, I need –

DOLORES. I'm sorry, Mr. Elwood, but I really must be – *(to* **MONA***)* I thought he'd seen me on TV, that maybe that was it, the TV…

JIM. Call me Jim. After all, we're connected, you and me.

DOLORES. Oh my, look at the time, I'm late.

JIM. You wore a white nightgown, a white…

*(***DOLORES** *freezes.)*

DOLORES. What?

JIM. Nightgown.

MONA. You should have screamed.

DOLORES. *(to* **MONA***)* I lost my voice, I could barely –

JIM. *(to* **RICHARD***)* I couldn't help myself. I couldn't get her out of my thoughts.

DOLORES. *(to* **JIM***)* Who are you what do you want from me?

JIM. I would never hurt you. Just…your name, tell me your name.

DOLORES. Dolores. *(to* **ELIOTT***)* I gave him my real name, I don't know why.

JIM. Dolores. Okay. You're all right. You're all right.

DOLORES. I'm fine. Now if you'll just –

JIM. I saw you in the nightgown. In the middle of the night, in the gown, in the white…I looked up.

DOLORES. Oh my God, you – oh my God.

RICHARD. And you waited to meet her? You staked her out?

DOLORES. You're the one who saw me. *(to* **MONA***)* He saw me. He saw me.

JIM. *(to* **RICHARD***)* I went to the building is all.

RICHARD. And she knows you?

JIM. I had to see her.

MONA. *(to* **DOLORES***)* He recognized you?

DOLORES. *(to* **MONA***)* Apparently, yes.

JIM. *(to* **DOLORES**, *grabbing her arm)* There is a connection. Between us. A connection. Do you understand what I'm talking about I think you do.

DOLORES. You're hurting me.

JIM. I love you. I love you, Dolores.

DOLORES. Oh my God.

RICHARD. You told her you loved her?

JIM. *(to* **RICHARD***)* I don't remember using the word "love."

ELIOTT. But of course what's love but an impulse to comfort, to help. To save…

JANINE. *(to* **ELIOTT***)* And if one doesn't need to be saved?

(**JIM** *hands* **DOLORES** *a gift: a white nightgown.*)

DOLORES. *(to* **MONA***)* He gave me a…*(to* **JIM***)* A nightgown?

JANINE. *(to* **ELIOTT***)* Can you love someone who doesn't need to be saved?

MONA. What do you mean a nightgown?

JIM. I'd like for you to wear it.

MONA. You didn't –

DOLORES. *(to* **MONA***)* He threatened me.

RICHARD. You threatened her?

JIM. *(to* **RICHARD***)* I didn't exactly threaten her. *(to* **DOLORES***)* Put on the nightgown.

DOLORES. *(to* **MONA***)* He had a gun.

(**JIM** *reveals a gun.*)

JIM. The nightgown – I need to see you in the nightgown. Put it on, dammit.

DOLORES. Good God.

JIM. It's just like the one you wore, right? The nightgown I saw you in? Please put on the nightgown.

DOLORES. You're sick. You need help. *(to* **ELIOTT***)* He needs –

ELIOTT. Help, yes.

DOLORES. HELP!

JIM. Please, Dolores. I need to see what I saw that night.

DOLORES. Oh God.

(She puts on the nightgown.)

JIM. My wife is leaving me. She wore sweats to bed. She always wore sweats. Like an armor. Suddenly I find little things around, those little…do you call them negligees? You were…this vision…there, this vision… floating over the river…I didn't know if the night had, if it had swallowed you "is she all right," I said. That's what stayed in my head, "is she all right." I suppose that's my training. I protect people. I keep them safe.

(holding the gun on her…)

JIM. You're safe with me. You feel safe, don't you?

RICHARD. This is bad, Jim.

JIM. We saw a woman fly up into the sky, Rich. Sucked up into the sky. Does this not in any way alter your brain? *(to* **DOLORES***)* Now run, Dolores. *(to* **RICHARD***)* Does this not affect you at *all*? *(to* **DOLORES***)* Please run.

DOLORES. Oh God…oh God. *(looks up)* What do you want from me? Why did you come to me, why did you choose me, why? There must be a reason. Isn't there?

JIM. Run faster. That's how it looked. Floating, floating in the night, RUN.

End of Act I

(**ELIOTT** *delivers a paper at a symposium.*)

ELIOTT. My many years of training in the field of analysis and the discrimination of aggrieved mental states did not prepare me for my encounters with abductees, or "experiencers," as I prefer to call them. As a psychiatrist, I have had to re-evaluate my notions of human woundedness. More exceptionally, we have in this one instance the corroboration of two outside witnesses. It becomes apparent that for the witnesses as well – the seers, as it were – the abduction event presents a serious trauma to the psyche. The spiritual and personal implications have proved to be quite unsettling, not just for her, but for all who have seen. Abduction phenomena present a radical challenge to the consensus reality. If the body is not what it seems, what are we? Who is this "I" standing before you? What are the larger questions? The questions we are afraid to address, because to live life with an awareness of these questions is a complication. Awareness can be a complication.

(DOLORES with MONA.)

MONA. You should press charges.

DOLORES. He didn't mean to hurt me.

MONA. He had a gun, Dee.

DOLORES. "The body is not what it seems."

MONA. He pointed a gun at your head. What did that feel like?

DOLORES. "The body is not what it seems."

MONA. Why do you keep you saying that?

DOLORES. It's something they say in UFO circles, something Eliott says. I'm not my body.

MONA. Hunh? What are you, then? Do you think I should go on a diet? Just a few pounds, but – look at me, Dolores. What do you think?

DOLORES. The body...the way it wants to be everything. The way we make it everything.

MONA. It says here that we're constantly shedding our skin. *(off magazine)* "Seventy percent of house dust consists of human skin." That's disgusting. That guy, the three-way, remember him? He meant another man. Can you believe that? Me and two *men*. Somehow that doesn't appeal to me. To be there for that. I thought he'd meant another woman. And now he's put that idea in my head – me and another woman – and the idea – it works for me, Dee.

(JIM and RICHARD)

JIM. I don't think I've ever been in love. Not really; really in love.

RICHARD. Let's try to stick to the relevant issues, Jim. You'll have to turn in your gun, I'm afraid. Have you done so?

(JIM hands over his gun.)

JIM. If I was, I can't remember it. Can't remember love.

RICHARD. Consider that a blessing. You didn't explain, I hope. No need to explain what cannot be explained.

JIM. Dammit, why?

RICHARD. Why what?

JIM. Why are we here, why?

RICHARD. Gee, Jim, I haven't asked that question since junior high school.

JIM. Why.

RICHARD. Snap out of it, Jim. *(beat)* It occurs to me that astronauts tend to have difficulty, upon their return. Because of the looking back part, apparently. The seeing the Earth part. To have that perspective, it must be very odd, I'd imagine. Your eyes are watering, Jim. A lot of pollen in the air this time of year. Here, you might want to wipe your eyes.

*(**DOLORES** on phone, looking up.)*

DOLORES. Tom? Tom, I know you're up there.
  So much has happened, Tom…I can't believe so much has happened without your even knowing.
  Your lights go on and off, you must be there.
  But maybe you aren't. Maybe it's someone else and –

*(**DOLORES** lets the phone receiver slide from her hand.)*

– and you're not inside at all.

*(**ELIOTT** in scene with **JIM**)*

ELIOTT. Being a witness can be even more of an ordeal than going through the experience oneself.

JIM. I've never had psychological problems. I'm not a weak person. Doctor. Should I call you Doctor?

ELIOTT. That's fine. This is your experience, as well. A violation of your reality.

JIM. I would never have hurt her, that was not my intention, to hurt.

ELIOTT. I must say that when I myself first began to understand what was going on, I was terrified, paralyzed almost. But then I thought – wonderful. Isn't it also wonderful?

JIM. How is she? How is she, Doctor, is she all right?

ELIOTT. You needn't be concerned about Dolores. Dolores is fine. We must focus on getting better yourself.

JIM. I need to keep her in front of me. If I can't keep her in front of me, I can't be sure she's all right.

ELIOTT. You know, Jim, I think it would be a good idea for you to rest somewhere. Jim?

JIM. Floating mid-air, and the more you try to stop the thought, the more it's there...

ELIOTT. I like to think of an institutional stay as taking a break from your thoughts. From your head. Because you mustn't contact her. Are we clear on that? I'm saying this for your own good. You must cut off contact. Do you understand?

JIM. Contact, right – to make contact. You people, when you use that word, it's like you have no idea. I mean Jesus Christ isn't that what we all want? To make – fucking – contact – with another – human being?

*(**MONA** in **ELIOTT**'s office)*

MONA. What happened is, I suddenly noticed this scar.

ELIOTT. May I see?

*(**MONA** extends her hand.)*

MONA. And I have this longing, too, this empty place, so I began to think that maybe this isn't something everyone has to feel. If I could understand it...

ELIOTT. You'd like to name it.

MONA. Yes. I do live right downstairs from her. We have the same view even. So I thought they might...since I am right downstairs. Because we are really similar, me and Dolores, don't you think?

*(**JANINE** holds a sketch pad as **DOLORES** speaks.)*

DOLORES. I couldn't see them at first, but I felt them. You know how someone staring at you in your sleep can make you wake up? I thought they were children at first. Their eyes were shaped like tears. That's what I'm seeing in my head. You're not going to draw this?

JANINE. I keep seeing the bad drawings, the cheesy pop drawings. You have an interesting face.

DOLORES. No, I don't. You think so?

JANINE. You should think better of yourself.

DOLORES. I've begun to. Really, I've begun to. To think more the way I did when I was a child. The letter x, I thought – in the dictionary? So few pages, so insignificant, like myself, and yet –

JANINE. Rare?

DOLORES. Special. The center – of something. Connected. To something. Does that sound stupid?

JANINE. No. I can see…

DOLORES. See what?

JANINE. Something in your face.

(JANINE goes to ELIOTT.)

JANINE. You want to sleep with her.

ELIOTT. What?

JANINE. Dolores. You want me to draw her "experience" so you can sleep with her through me.

ELIOTT. But we're not sleeping together, Janine, so that equation doesn't quite make sense.

JANINE. "Make sense." Do those words mean anything to you anymore? But I suppose it's no longer my concern; whom you desire and so forth.

ELIOTT. If you're talking about transference, counter-transference –

JANINE. "Transference," such a nice term. So polite. As if a label justifies – or reduces, I should say, reduces a feeling to a category. An acceptable, non-threatening *category*, but isn't it just the feeling between two people who are sitting in a room together and want to fuck each other's brains out?

(RICHARD enters scene with DOLORES and MONA.)

RICHARD. I can imagine that you must have been disturbed. By such behavior.

MONA. Of course she was.

DOLORES. It was disturbing, yes.

RICHARD. He's been my partner for a long time and this has all been very difficult. The seeing, and so on.

MONA. The guy is totally nuts.

RICHARD. Jim's taken a leave, so, you won't have to worry about Jim.

DOLORES. Yes, I…It's important to have been witnessed. It's important that you both came forward.

MONA. He didn't find anything when he hypnotized me. Eliott didn't. I thought since I live right downstairs and, well, nothing came up. Apparently I kept talking about the swimming pool we had when I was a kid. before my parents got divorced. That was a good year, the year of the swimming pool.

(They look at her.)

So what business are you in exactly? Protection, did you say?

RICHARD. Security, yes.

MONA. I could use some of that.

DOLORES. Mona?

MONA. I better go to work. *(She gets up to go.)* You're – ?

DOLORES. It's okay.

MONA. I'm right downstairs, and, um, maybe you can come by after and check my lock? I don't always feel safe. I guess a locksmith is a whole different thing, but you probably know about that stuff, right?

RICHARD. Not really.

MONA. Oh, okay, then. See ya.

(MONA goes. A pause.)

RICHARD. You're a very attractive woman.

DOLORES. Oh.

RICHARD. I would be a liar to say that I don't have feelings, too. To pretend that this incident did not somehow inspire feelings.

DOLORES. Feelings?

RICHARD. There. Good. I feel better having said that. I came here to apologize for Jim, to tell you that you're safe from Jim, and I...I...Will you kiss me, Dolores?

DOLORES. What?

RICHARD. I'm sorry, I don't know what's – but a kiss, what's a kiss, so innocent –

DOLORES. A kiss is the most intimate thing.

RICHARD. You think so?

DOLORES. By far, yes. Face to face. And so on. Face to face.

RICHARD. Oh boy, I really didn't intend – it's my opinion as a professional that you're in a highly vulnerable situation.

DOLORES. We all are.

RICHARD. I could take a leave of absence from the company. I could offer you my services at no charge.

DOLORES. No one can "protect" me.

RICHARD. Dammit, you *need* me, Dolores. Did you know that I was in the military?

DOLORES. I can believe that.

RICHARD. I was in a highly sensitive top-secret area I can't say what.

DOLORES. All right.

RICHARD. You probably want to know.

DOLORES. I'm fine not knowing.

RICHARD. But you must be curious. I was. I never knew. I left because I am not a military man in certain respects. I am not a government man. I do not like fitting into someone else's agenda when the mission is not made clear. Intentions were kept from me. I was used in this respect. Fuck that.

DOLORES. I know the feeling.

RICHARD. Pardon my language. You do?

DOLORES. The feeling of being kept in the dark about how you're being used.

RICHARD. I collect flea market photos. Sort of a hobby of mine, if I were to have a hobby.

DOLORES. Hunh.

RICHARD. Old family albums, that sort of thing. They look out at you. The people in the photos. It's like they're looking straight at you, without even knowing who you are. They're all dead now, of course, and I, I'm not quite comfortable looking real people in the eye like that. I don't want to intrude, I suppose.

DOLORES. And yet –

RICHARD. Well, right, it must seem…Let me tell you something, Dolores, do you mind if I call you Dolores? We've been thrown together, the three of us, by this vision we've shared. Of course there's a dynamic here, being that we two saw you, and you didn't see us, so, so as you know Jim is having trouble with, er, reality. He's convinced of what he saw.

DOLORES. "Convinced"?

RICHARD. Please forgive me if I'm being forward but is it possible that, like my friend Jim, you have a fragile constitution?

DOLORES. What?

RICHARD. I would not hold that against you. I would even find it very attractive.

DOLORES. Please, I…please –

RICHARD. You live on the fourteenth floor. That's very high up. Surprisingly high. What, a hundred-and-forty-three feet? You have a balcony – standing on that balcony, in the darkness, in a white nightgown – on a windy night and – if you had just leaned over the edge –

DOLORES. I would never lean over the edge.

RICHARD. For a moment, let's say – an illusion could have been created –

DOLORES. I'm afraid of heights. I've always been afraid that the balcony would fall – that it would break, so I would never even be out on it –

RICHARD. Looking at this balcony, at it's position and so forth, I can't help noting that you might have gone out there, you might have even been asleep, walking in your sleep; it was a warm night, you wanted air – and you appeared in such a way that we could not see what was holding you up. Isn't it possible?

DOLORES. You were there, my God. You saw me. You *said* you saw me.

RICHARD. I could have been mistaken. I don't know what I saw. The sky if filled with all kinds of optical effects. You realize that? Anyone who spends any amount of time at all watching a night sky will tell you that. Optical effects that have labels, even, scientific labels because these effects are understood scientifically. And Jim, Jim is clearly not well. The power of suggestion is an amazing thing.

DOLORES. You can't change what you saw.

RICHARD. Do you even remember? Do you really remember?

(**RICHARD** *goes.*)

DOLORES. I'm chosen, now. I'm chosen, and I'm a part of this. My body remembers. My body remembers, not just my head. There's a memory in my body, a scar, you can't invent that.

(**DOLORES** *looks up.*)

I'm ready now. Why don't you come back to me?

(**DOLORES** *goes to phone.*)

Come back.

(**DOLORES** *and* **MONA** *in a bar.*)

MONA. Vodka gimlet.

DOLORES. Glass of red wine, please. All these women…

MONA. Why does it bring tears to my eyes to see a bar full of women, only women? Not sad tears, though. Not at all sad.

DOLORES. The body is not what it seems.

MONA. Where are you going? I'm not here to pick anybody up. I just want to know if I'll be noticed. By these women. If anybody will watch me. *(downs the drink)* Watch me.

(**JANINE** *displays large canvases to* **ELIOTT**.)

JANINE. The male gaze…I suppose that's what it's about. In my work, I'm sometimes accused of pornography but you see as women we objectify our*selves*, not the male body…our own bodies. Such is the cultural message. Nine out of ten straight women prefer looking at pictures of naked women to naked men. That's an estimate, I made that up, but…in my experience. And why is that? The turn-on is to BE the object, to identify with the object…looking at pictures of naked women we become both viewer *and* object. We co-opt the male gaze as our own, and turn it upon ourselves.

I guess that's it.

ELIOTT. I still think it's pornographic.

JANINE. Oh, screw you, El.

ELIOTT. Beautiful, but a little…

JANINE. What? Arousing? You're aroused? *(beat)* You know you were never supportive of my work, never. You never understood what I was trying to do.

ELIOTT. I would honestly like to understand. That's why I'm asking you.

JANINE. I just explained, something I hate to do, and I just did.

ELIOTT. That's the part in your head. What I've never understood is the impulse underneath, the need to display yourself –

JANINE. Oh, screw you; don't psychoanalyze me, screw you.

(**JANINE** *takes down her canvases, starts to roll them up.*)

ELIOTT. Remember when I got tenure, how happy I was?

JANINE. If you're going to tell me they may take it away, I've heard already.

ELIOTT. It's under review.

JANINE. You had to expect.

ELIOTT. That was a good time, really. To have one thing like that, one thing that I wanted. One thing that would be enough.

JANINE. It's what *we* wanted. Me the good little wife; that's all I wanted, too.

ELIOTT. You were having an affair.

JANINE. Because I thought you were. Because I thought I was losing you. Because I was losing you, in fact.

ELIOTT. The other way around, in fact.

JANINE. And I knew when I would finally break down and tell you – and of course I finally did tell you – I knew you would look at me impassively, with total understanding actually, with absolutely no jealousy or rage or passion and you would say:

ELIOTT. I understand, Janine.

JANINE. "I understand." And I would say. "Fuck you and your understanding and –" Goddamn it, it isn't ever over, is it. You can always peel away the surface and find it, the painful little nicks, the bloody things.

ELIOTT. I understand.

(She starts to go.)

Do you think it's strange that neither of us went on to have children?

JANINE. More children, you mean.

ELIOTT. More, yes. Do you think of him?

JANINE. I don't need to talk about this now. I'm sorry, it should have been before, not now. The past is past. It should be kept in a box, like an old photograph. That's why people save things in a box, isn't it? So they can forget them. Know they're there, then forget.

*(**RICHARD** visits **JIM**.)*

RICHARD. You're okay. You've been working hard is all. Eighty percent of American adults suffer symptoms of stress and fatigue. Read that in *Newsweek*. What I'm saying, Jim, what I'm saying is what you're going through is not unusual. I'm sure this whole thing will blow over.

JIM. Have you *heard* anything.

RICHARD. Try not to think too much.

JIM. Is she all *right*.

RICHARD. Don't worry about her, Jim. She's fine. Apparently. She didn't press charges, so. So I'm sure she's all right.

JIM. We protect people. We make them feel safe. That is our job. What are we protecting them from, Richard? What? From dangers. From dangers. Why are there dangers?

RICHARD. I don't know, Jim. There are bad people in the world. Some people are bad. It's our job to keep those bad people from important people. That's a good job. A satisfying job. A job you can wake up every morning and feel good about. I re-filed the report, Jim. They'd asked were we drunk. Were we drunk, Jim. They had the nerve to ask that.

JIM. He was in that building screwing someone.

RICHARD. It's not our concern what he was doing.

JIM. He was in that building getting fucked.

RICHARD. What he was doing is irrelevant.

JIM. While we protected him.

RICHARD. He's an important person.

JIM. We stood outside waiting like two dumb fucks.

RICHARD. I resent that. He may be obscure to us but he's politically important.

JIM. *(calmly)* You had to whiz.

RICHARD. His dealings are of great consequence.

JIM. I looked up.

RICHARD. We don't know what he was doing.

JIM. You looked up, too.

RICHARD. He could have been doing anything. The course of nations is influenced by this man. The course of *nations*.

JIM. It was the middle of the night. He had us wait outside. We protected a man while he was getting –

RICHARD. We don't know this.

JIM. And we looked up... *Something* made us look up.

RICHARD. I went back to the building as well. I went back in daylight. I will tell you what I saw. I saw a building with balconies. At night was this even apparent? We did not see them on the night in question. Does this mean said balconies are not in fact there? Do said balconies not exist because the night renders them invisible to the human eye? No, of course not, thus... we did not necessarily see what we saw. Narrow little balconies with dark metal railings that would be difficult if not impossible to see at night, on a dark night. Juliet balconies, I think they're called. Now if a person were standing on one of these balconies at night, you might see only the person. Not the thing upon which the person was standing. We must re-evaluate, Jim. We must in fact reevaluate what it is that we believe we saw. I've re-evaluated, Jim. I've rewritten the report, Jim.

JIM. You son-of-a-bitch.

RICHARD. A woman leaning over her balcony. A woman in a white nightgown. White. *(pulling himself out of the vision)* There is no problem. There is no situation. The woman in question is safe.

JIM. She's "safe."

(DOLORES sits for JANINE. Very still. JANINE draws her.)

DOLORES. Parts. Pieces of my body. I never thought of it that way.

JANINE. I always have.

DOLORES. Do you like looking at me?

JANINE. Yes, I do.

DOLORES. You're not getting bored with me yet?

JANINE. No.

DOLORES. Tell me if I move too much. Do you know what you want to do with me yet?

JANINE. I'm just drawing.

DOLORES. Will you tear up the pictures – cut them up – the way you did the ones of yourself?

JANINE. That's what I usually do. With the pictures. Tear them up and put them back together somehow, that's what I do.

DOLORES. This man – Tom – Eliott didn't tell you about Tom, did he? The person I used to see?

JANINE. No, he wouldn't have.

DOLORES. His name was Tom. (Of course his name still *is* Tom.) He stopped wanting me. Stopped wanting my body. "It's not you," he said. "Not you." But who was it, then? I don't know why that's been the hardest part to admit. He had a pair of reading glasses that had broke, that were Scotch-taped together. The frame held together by Scotch tape. When he wore those glasses I always felt so sad. And so full of love. So sad and so full of love…

Do the people who sit for you, do they often find themselves – talking like this?

JANINE. I usually draw myself.

DOLORES. You must think of things. When you draw? What do you think of?

JANINE. I just look.

DOLORES. But your mind must wander sometimes…What was it like being married to Eliott? Sorry, what a stupid question.

JANINE. It was years ago.

DOLORES. At least he hasn't disappeared. I find that the hardest. When they're there, and then they're not.

(JANINE *continues to draw. Silence for a moment.*)

JANINE. Eliott and I had a child. He lived for 18 days. Tiny, in the incubator, we never got to take him home. *Name him*, they said. I didn't want to have to hold onto that: a name.

DOLORES. I'm sorry.

JANINE. They gave us a photograph. A picture we could keep of our child, we couldn't take him home, so – (*stops herself*) I'm sorry, what is wrong with me, talking to you this way.

DOLORES. I'm glad, really.

JANINE. "Dolores." Doesn't that mean pain in Spanish, something like that? Maybe we should stop for the day.

*(**DOLORES** relaxes her pose.)*

DOLORES. It's exhausting. Remaining so still. I wouldn't have thought that.

JANINE. It's very hard work, I tried to warn you. To be the sitter – it's not at all passive, as one might suppose.

DOLORES. Do you miss him still?

JANINE. Eliott?

DOLORES. Your son. Sorry, I shouldn't –

JANINE. You have no children?

DOLORES. No. I feel it, though. A child somewhere, a child that's mine. It makes no sense, I haven't had one.

JANINE. I won't have another.

*(**ELIOTT** enters scene with **JANINE**.)*

ELIOTT. She what?

JANINE. She sat for me, yes.

ELIOTT. I wanted you to paint a memory. To make a concrete illustration of her memory of an event. Not paint her naked, not make her part of you…whatever it is you do. Was she naked?

JANINE. That's not the issue.

ELIOTT. I think it is. She's my patient.

JANINE. You said you don't have patients anymore. You're working on your book. You're doing research.

ELIOTT. Research with people who, who are in essence my patients. Don't use her to get back at me.

JANINE. You know you're very lucky to have kept your tenure.

ELIOTT. You don't think I should have?

JANINE. What you're doing, I don't think it's rigorous. Flying saucers?

ELIOTT. Jung wrote about them.

JANINE. As visual rumors. As metaphors. I'm sorry, but I just find your work a little...shall I say "pornographic"?

ELIOTT. You want her to sit for you, why is that? Why Dolores? I'll tell you why. Because of her experience. You sense it, too. It's real, and it's changed her, and we all want to be part of it.

JANINE. I have an image in my head, that's all. An image in my head that I think she can fulfill. Like you, I manipulate for my own purposes. Just like you.

ELIOTT. When she came to me she didn't have the story. The story *emerged*.

JANINE. *Stories* tend to.

ELIOTT. And the others like her...I've seen so many others now. All these people who come to me, it can't be a coincidence.

JANINE. It's not a coincidence. It's your own design.

ELIOTT. When she came to me she was like a glass that had been shattered; she couldn't hold anything.

JANINE. My point precisely.

ELIOTT. Now she heals. We found the glue so she can *heal*.

JANINE. And Truth doesn't matter?

ELIOTT. This is Truth. I'm helping people. Whatever you may think, I help.

JANINE. I think...I think this is like the time you spilled the punch bowl onto my white dress.

ELIOTT. What punch bowl?

JANINE. The summer after we met...I was still in grad school, I was wearing a new white cotton dress, very simple, the one with the eyelets along here, remember? And you spilled the punch right on me, trying to serve me a cup, don't you remember?

ELIOTT. No, I don't. What are you talking about?

JANINE. How can you not remember that? You were so embarrassed...hating to be so clumsy, I suppose...then you had to wipe my dress but it was rather in the wrong place for that, I couldn't stop laughing...don't you remember?

ELIOTT. I don't know, it was ages ago, the summer after we met.

JANINE. The day of the faculty party...you were nervous having me there...and then, of course, when the whole punch bowl dumped onto the ground, you looked so surprised...

(She's laughing.)

Remember now?

ELIOTT. Maybe. Possibly. A lot's happened since then and now...okay, yes, so I spilled punch on you, that sounds familiar, what is your point, Janine?

JANINE. My point? My point is that the whole punch thing ...it never happened, darling. I made it up.

*(**JANINE** goes.)*

*(**DOLORES** on her toes, reaching, hypnotized as before.)*

ELIOTT. I'm going to bring you back there. I'm going to bring you to the first time. Can you go back to the first time with me?

DOLORES. I think so.

ELIOTT. Let's find the first time together. You won't be afraid anymore?

DOLORES. I'm not afraid. They're looking at me. I'm not afraid.

ELIOTT. You see the eyes?

DOLORES. Yes. They're watching me. Large eyes...infant eyes but so large.

ELIOTT. And what do they see?

DOLORES. Me. My body. I am...I am inside my body.

ELIOTT. What do they want from you, Dolores?

DOLORES. My body. They want a body. They want another body.

ELIOTT. It's okay...keep going, you're safe...who, Dolores? Tell me who.

DOLORES. I can see their eyes...eyes of a child, I think... infant eyes...Tom's eyes, Tom's eyes when he was a child...

ELIOTT. Tom?

DOLORES. Tom's eyes…my mother's eyes…my father…I see my father watching me, somebody watching me… you, your eyes…I don't know who they are, I don't know what they want from me…

ELIOTT. What do you see, Dolores? What? What do you remember? WHAT?

(**DOLORES** *turns to* **MONA**.)

MONA. You're saying it isn't true?

DOLORES. I don't know. It feels true.

MONA. You have witnesses. One witness, anyway.

DOLORES. There it is, like a snapshot, something you look at and then it's inside your head like it was always your own. But maybe it wasn't.

MONA. He saw you, Dee. You were seen.

(**DOLORES** *visits* **JIM**.)

DOLORES. That night, when you saw me – what did you see?

JIM. You. I saw you. UFOs. I can't say for sure that's what I thought at the time. I didn't know what. A woman floating, floating over the river. A Madonna…an offering. You were there. And then you weren't. And it made no sense, no sense at all. "A woman is floating up in the air," I thought. "My God," I thought.

DOLORES. How could it have been a dream, unless we were all having the same dream at once?

JIM. A dream? I have never seen another person so clearly. So bright against the sky. The sky was dark, and you were so bright against it.

DOLORES. I've been a stalker, too. I had to see him; no, to be seen by him. If he saw me, we'd connect again, we'd have to connect.

JIM. My wife won't visit me. She thinks we were having an affair or something, you and me. She's been having one, so.

DOLORES. It's such a joke, Cupid slinging all these arrows in the wrong direction.

JIM. You were always safe with me.

DOLORES. I don't think I'll be able to visit you again.

JIM. I can understand.

(with surprise)

I held a gun to your head.

DOLORES. But I was safe.

*(**DOLORES** crosses into a sheet of light. She tilts her face into it and is suddenly happy for a moment. The happiness takes her by surprise.)*

*(**DOLORES** crosses to **ELIOTT**.)*

DOLORES. I was happy, you know. This afternoon, on my way over here? Just – happy.

ELIOTT. Tell me.

DOLORES. It took me by surprise. It wasn't anything. It wasn't Tom or anyone or anything. I was just crossing the street when I got stuck midway, on the median. Just a little grassy strip with traffic whizzing by me in both directions. All of a sudden the light shifted, just a notch…it must have been exactly the right angle… the way the sunlight caught the buildings, and landed on the strip of grass. Everything connected to everything. I turned my face into the light and everything stopped, and was perfect, and I know what it is to feel that now.

ELIOTT. When I was a little boy – my mother used to love to tell this story – well, she had just explained to me about God, this notion of God. "Where *is* God?" I said. "God is everywhere, all the time." "But why is God here all the time?" I asked. "We only need him at night."

(They look at each other.)

DOLORES. I hope it's good, what they want from us. I hope there's something out there, and it's good.

ELIOTT. I'm glad we…

DOLORES. Made contact?

ELIOTT. Made contact, right.

(**JIM** *and* **RICHARD** *stand guard, back on duty.*)

RICHARD. Now remember, Jim, this is a very important person we're protecting.

JIM. I know this.

RICHARD. We can't let anything happen. You're still on probation.

JIM. Don't worry about me.

RICHARD. It is good to have you back. Don't look up, though.

JIM. Right.

RICHARD. Just don't look up.

(**DOLORES** *in her apartment with* **MONA**.)

DOLORES. I won't ever hear from him again.

MONA. You're not still thinking about Tom, are you?

DOLORES. Do you think he's seeing someone new?

MONA. Not so new anymore.

DOLORES. I don't miss him anymore.

I miss the way I used to miss him. I try to picture his face. It comes in pieces, all scotch-taped together, like the glasses he wore. All broken, and just barely put back together.

MONA. He was a mess.

(**JIM** *and* **RICHARD**, *still on duty.*)

JIM. It was beautiful, though. You gotta admit, to get to see something like that?

RICHARD. A beautiful illusion.

JIM. Okay, Rich.

RICHARD. I wish I had pictures of me when I was a boy.

JIM. What's that?

RICHARD. Pictures, photographs. Of my childhood. I don't have any. I don't know where they are. If anyone saved them. Do you have pictures of yourself from when you were a kid?

JIM. Sure. My mother has them. I guess. She gave one to my wife, she probably threw it out. It doesn't really matter though, does it?

RICHARD. I guess not. I thought I might like to have them.

JIM. Yeah, well, it doesn't really matter. Do you believe in God, Rich?

RICHARD. That's a personal question, Jim.

JIM. Right. You're right. I guess it is.

*(***DOLORES*** still in her apartment with ***MONA***. ***MONA*** *flips through a magazine.)*

MONA. Do you not love the Danbury Mint collection? These miniatures they make…it's incredible, what they can do. "The Enchanted Castle," look at this. It's five inches tall. Isn't it perfect?

DOLORES. What are you supposed to do with it?

MONA. You collect them, Dee.

DOLORES. *(looking at balcony)* I never go out on my balcony, do I?

MONA. They're just so…perfect.

DOLORES. It's so small, and I've never trusted that it wouldn't crumble beneath me.

MONA. It's pretty beautiful, isn't it? To take something so big and make it teeny tiny? I love that.

*(***DOLORES*** moves toward the balcony.)*

DOLORES. I was upset that night. That was the worst time. I loved Tom and he loved me and suddenly he didn't. I couldn't make sense of that. He had loved me, and then he didn't anymore; chose me, then unchose me. I couldn't get over that. *(to* **MONA***)* He was a chubby little boy, Tom was. He showed me a picture and I thought: that's my child. That's my boy. Then I loved him more.

MONA. Forget Tom. I want this castle.

DOLORES. I was possessed, wasn't I?

MONA. You mean obsessed? A perfect re-creation, but tiny. I love it.

(**DOLORES** *stands. Out of body, unheard by* **MONA**. **MONA** *continues to address her as if she's sitting beside her.*)

DOLORES. *(to herself)* I never go out on my balcony but that night, that night I might have.

MONA. Monthly installments. I'm going to send away.

DOLORES. Might have opened the glass doors to stand, and look – down. Might have wanted the ground to crumble beneath me. I can't say for sure that I didn't. It was the middle of the night. I was sleeping, or awake only briefly. I remember the breeze.

(**DOLORES** *moves toward the balcony.*)

MONA. Do you think 29.99 a month is too expensive?

DOLORES. *(to* **MONA***)* How many months? *(to herself)* I remember the breeze. And the lights from the bridge. My nightgown fluttering around me.

MONA. Four, I think…four installments.

DOLORES. *(to* **MONA***)* If you love it, you should get it.

DOLORES. *(to herself)* "The body is not what it seems."

MONA. Yeah. I should.

DOLORES. *(to herself)* I remember the pain – if it's possible to remember pain. Maybe it isn't.

MONA. I think if I could have this castle…the whole collection, maybe, all these perfect little places…I could build a shelf for them. In my bedroom? I think I could be happy, having this shelf of perfect little places to look at all the time…

(**DOLORES** *goes out onto the balcony.*)

DOLORES. I didn't want it anymore…my body. My body was heavy, and tired, and then I…I looked up. I'd been looking down, down at the river, but something made me look up instead…the stars, the night, light. The light is so bright in the sky at night, so much out there and so…bright.

(**MONA** *still talks to* **DOLORES** *as if she's beside her.*)

MONA. Something else…something more…

DOLORES. I felt so light I could hardly keep my feet planted; so light I could float "the body is not what it seems…"

MONA. …there must be.

DOLORES. I see myself floating in mid-air in the white nightgown. How is it that I can see myself? I see myself falling, but I'm standing here. "The body is not what it seems, the body –"

*(Lights fade out on **MONA** as she reaches out to **DOLORES** in the empty seat. **DOLORES** steps onto the balcony, released from the body she's left behind her.)*

DOLORES. – is not what it seems." I see myself leaning over a balcony, but I'm not leaning, so how can I see that? I see that night but that night is gone so how is it that I can hold it…like a photograph. I see Tom's face but he's not here, and won't be again, so what does it mean to see that? I see my self Scotch-taped together, like a pair of broken glasses…

Pieces of me have been floating away into the darkness and I think it's me I'm trying to grab hold of…I think it's me hovering over the water, about to fall… *not* falling…imagining myself somewhere else and not knowing, not knowing how to get there.

(A solitary woman in a white nightgown in the darkness.)

Please God let me remember this. Will I remember this? Because I want, I want to remember.

*(**DOLORES** turns her face to a bright, bold light. Blackout.)*

End of Play

ABOUT THE AUTHOR

NEENA BEBER's plays include *Jump/Cut, A Common Vision, The Dew Point, Hard Feelings* (Ojai Playwrights Conference), *Tomorrowland* (New Gorges; Theatre J in Washington D.C.), *Failure to Thrive, The Course of It, The Brief but Exemplary Life of the Living Goddess* (Magic Theatre) and *Misreadings* (ATL's Humana Festival, published in *The Best American Short Plays 1997*). *Thirst*, commissioned by Otterbein College, has been developed in The Public Theatre's New Work Now, Seattle's ACT, Williamstown Theatre Festival, and HBO's Stage to Screen. Other plays have premiered at Padua Playwrights Festival, circus minimus, Soho Rep, Watermark Theatre, En Garde Arts, and City Theatre, among other places. A.S.K. Exchange to the Royal Court Theatre, Distinguished Alumni Award from NYU's Tisch School of the Arts, member of New Dramatists. Short film: *Bad Dates*, based on her one act *Fool*. She has received Emmy and Ace-Award nominations for her writing for television, and has contributed plays to the 52nd Street Project. She is the recipient of Paulette Goddard and MacDowell Colony Fellowships.

**Also by
Neena Beber...**

Tomorrowland

Jump/Cut

The Dew Point

Please visit our website **samuelfrench.com** for complete descriptions and licensing information.

OTHER TITLES AVAILABLE FROM SAMUEL FRENCH

JUMP/CUT
Neena Beber

Little Theatre / Drama / 2m, 1f / Unit Set

Three bright urbanites want to make their mark on the world. Paul, a master of irony and distance, is a hardworking film maker on the rise. His girlfriend Karen, a grad student, must get on with her thesis or find a life outside of academia. Dave, a life long buddy whose brilliance is being consumed by increasingly severe episodes of manic depression, is camping on Paul's couch. Paul and Karen decide to turn Paul into a documentary. The camera is on 24 hours a day, capturing up close images of his jags and torpors and their responses. How far will love, friendship and ambition take this hip trio?

SAMUELFRENCH.COM

OTHER TITLES AVAILABLE FROM SAMUEL FRENCH

THE DEW POINT
Neena Beber

Dramatic Comedy / 2m, 3f

Can a woman be friends with a womanizer – even if she once dated him herself? And if your best friend wants to date the guy, do you stand in her way? *The Dew Point* is a play about love and marriage, sex and friendship, authenticity and blackmail...and the lies we tell in order to stay honest.

"...A comedy of sexual manners whose characters are funny yet sympathetic and complexly believable...The success of this deceptively labeled "romantic comedy" lies in the way it zeroes in on the way we deceive others by deceiving ourselves, plumping the bread of friendship into some pretty rancid sandwiches that are, of course, proffered with the best of intentions."
– Carolyn Clay, *Boston Phoenix*

"It is a pleasure to report that *The Dew Point* by Neena Beber, who won a *Village Voice* OBIE last season for emerging playwright, is an intelligent, well constructed, contemporary drama with sharp, bright, witty dialogue and fully detailed vibrant, believeable characters."
– Bob Rendell, *Talkin' Broadway*

SAMUELFRENCH.COM

www.ingramcontent.com/pod-product-compliance
Lightning Source LLC
Chambersburg PA
CBHW070650300426
44111CB00013B/2354